ECOSYSTEMS
and
FOOD CHAINS

Troll Associates

ECOSYSTEMS
and
FOOD CHAINS

by Francene Sabin

Illustrated by Art Cumings

Troll Associates

Library of Congress Cataloging in Publication Data

Sabin, Francene.
    Ecosystems and food chains.

    Summary: Explains the natural patterns by which plants
and animals depend upon each other and the environment
for food, and emphasizes the dangers of pesticides and
other human interference with the ecosystem.
    1. Ecology—Juvenile literature.   2. Food chains
(Ecology)—Juvenile literature.   [1. Ecology.   2. Food
chains (Ecology)]   1. Cumings, Art, ill.   II. Title.
QH541.14.S23   1985   574.5   84-2707
ISBN 0-8167-0282-9 (lib. bdg.)
ISBN 0-8167-0283-7 (pbk.)

As the ocean waves lap at the sandy beach, a sea gull swoops down and snares a crab washed ashore by the tide. In the dark forest, a squirrel leaps from tree to tree, its cheeks bulging with food, while a white-tailed deer nibbles the leaves on a shrub.

In the desert, the blazing sun beats down on the hot, dry sands, and a snake coils in the shade of a prickly cactus plant. At a faraway pond, a frog sits like a statue on a lily pad, until its sticky tongue lashes out and captures a passing mosquito. And out on the flat, open prairie, fields of golden grain sway in the soft summer breeze.

The ocean, the forest, the desert, the pond, and the prairie are very different from each other. The plants and animals that live in them are different, too. But all of them are important ecosystems in our world. An ecosystem is the relationship of plants and animals with each other and with the environment in which they live.

Some ecosystems are very large. An ocean is the largest kind of ecosystem. Some ecosystems are very small. A pond surrounded by fields and woods is a very small ecosystem.

But no matter how large or how small they are, all ecosystems work in the same way. The plants and animals in them fill each other's needs in a never-ending cycle of life.

It all begins with the sun. Without the sun, no green plants could exist. And without green plants, no animal life could exist. The green plants are called primary producers. Using the sun's energy, they turn water and a gas called carbon dioxide into simple sugar, which they need in order to grow.

The green plants, called primary producers, are eaten by many kinds of animals. These animals are the primary consumers. There are many different kinds of primary consumers.

For example, in the water, fish and other animals eat tiny green plants called algae. In meadows and pastures, cows and other grazing animals eat grass. At the edge of a field, a mouse eats grain. And in the forest, a squirrel eats acorns.

All of these animals are primary consumers who eat the food made by food-producing plants. When you eat fruits or vegetables or cereals, you are a primary consumer!

The relationship between the plants and the animals that eat them is called a food chain. The plant-animal relationship is the simplest kind of food chain. There are only two links: primary producer and primary consumer.

There are also longer food chains, however. When a mouse eats grain, and an owl then eats the mouse, it is a food chain with three links. These links are: primary producer, primary consumer, and secondary consumer. The grain is the primary producer. The mouse is the primary consumer, and the owl is the secondary consumer.

When people eat meat—such as beef—they are secondary consumers in a food chain that includes meadow grass, beef cattle, and people.

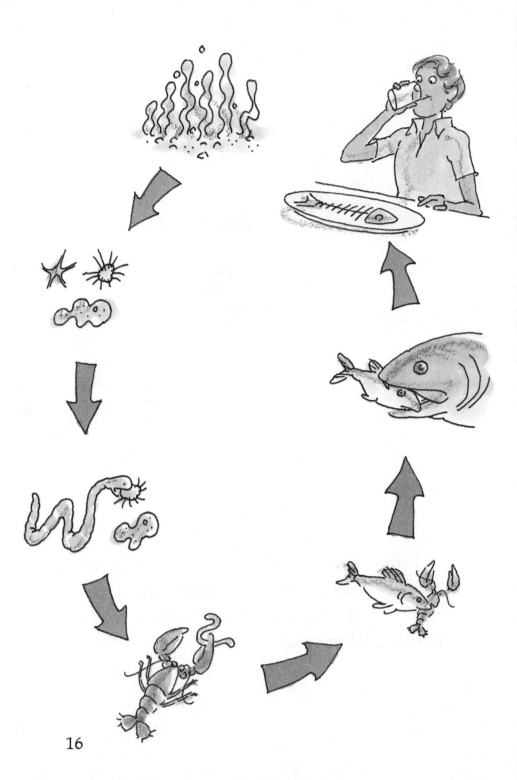

Some of the food we eat involves a very long food chain. One example of this might be a person eating a kind of fish called a bass.

Before being caught, the bass grew fat in the water by feeding on smaller fish called minnows. These minnows had eaten the larvae, or partly developed form, of crayfish. The crayfish, or lobster-like shellfish, had eaten the larvae of insects.

The insects, in turn, had eaten tiny, one-celled organisms called protozoa. And the protozoa had eaten algae, the green plants in the water. So, from the original food-producing algae to the person eating the fish, there is a food chain with seven links.

The person who eats the fish is at the top of this particular food chain. He or she is also at the top of a food pyramid. Like all pyramids, it has a broad base, and it gets narrower and narrower until it comes to a point at the top.

At the top of the pyramid is one person. That person may have eaten many fish. Those fish are beneath the person in the pyramid. Beneath the fish are the many minnows they had eaten. Beneath the minnows are the hundreds of crayfish larvae they ate.

The crayfish larvae ate thousands of insect larvae, which themselves ate millions of protozoa. And each protozoa cell ate a vast number of algae. The countless food-producing algae are at the base, or bottom, of the food pyramid.

The person who eats the fish, is, in a way, eating much, much more. The person is consuming minnows, crayfish larvae, and so on, down to the algae at the bottom of the pyramid. Obviously, it takes a great number of algae, protozoa, larvae, and minnows to put even one fish on a plate.

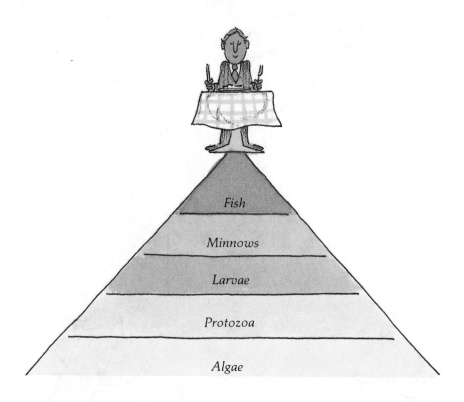

Fish

Minnows

Larvae

Protozoa

Algae

A steer must eat more than two pounds of grain to produce enough meat for one hamburger. You probably couldn't eat two pounds of corn or wheat in one sitting, but you wouldn't find it hard to eat one hamburger!

Each time you eat a hamburger you are a link in one food chain. When you eat fish, you are a link in another food chain. When you eat roast turkey or pork chops or applesauce, you are a link in still other food chains. Each food chain may seem to be separate from all the others, but they really are all tied together in a very large and complex "food web."

Imagine that you are in the center of a web, like a spider. The strand of the web that is closest to you is made up of all the foods you eat. Spreading out from that strand are many other strands.

One is the food chain that became your hamburger. Another is the food chain that became the fish. Still another is an applesauce apple that grew on a tree after an apple blossom was pollinated by a bee. And on and on. The web that surrounds you is very complicated. That is because a food web connects many food chains.

People eat a great variety of foods produced in many different ecosystems. In order to keep that supply of food plentiful, we must keep the ecosystems healthy.

Fruit

Potatoes

Fish

Bread

Cereal

Meat

Pie

Juice

Corn

Milk

23

For example, if the ecosystem of the prairie was destroyed by drought or flood, there would not be enough grain. And without grain there could be no bread or cereal for us to eat. Without grain there would also be no food for grain-eating animals. And this would mean that there would be no meat.

Sometimes an ecosystem is destroyed by something that happens very far away from it. This kind of destruction can begin with a pesticide being sprayed on farm land. All the insects that threaten the crops may be killed by the pesticide. But even after the crops are harvested, the pesticide may remain on the ground.

Suppose the pesticide is effective for a long time. When the spring rains wash it into nearby streams, these streams carry the pesticide into rivers. All along the way, the pesticide reaches different forms of life, including insects. Some of these insects may also be wiped out by the chemical. This cuts down the food supply for the fish and birds that feed on them.

The effect of the pesticide doesn't necessarily end there. The rivers may carry the pesticide all the way to the sea. And all along the way the balance of nature is being upset, and ecosystems are being harmed.

The ecosystem that is the ocean may be thousands of miles from the ecosystem where the pesticide was sprayed, but the two distant ecosystems are as closely linked as if they were next to each other.

If it is not disturbed by harmful sub-stances, an ecosystem can continue its cycle of life for a very long time. In a healthy pond, plants and animals remain in the pond's food web even when they die.

They fall to the muddy bottom, where they start to decompose, or break down. The minerals they contained go into the water, into new plants, into protozoa, and into the soil. In this way, the minerals remain within the pond's life cycle and keep it healthy.

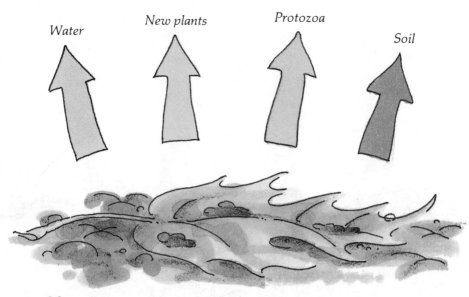

Water *New plants* *Protozoa* *Soil*

Live and dead material

In time, a pond may become clogged with so much living and dead material that it fills up and becomes land. As this slowly happens, the ecosystem of the pond changes to a marsh ecosystem, and then to a prairie ecosystem. And from a prairie ecosystem— if tree seeds take root—a forest ecosystem may develop.

This change, or succession, of ecosystems is part of the Earth's natural pattern. It is slow and gradual, but in time, it can bring about surprising changes.

In time, a white-tailed deer may nibble tender leaves where once a heron waded knee-deep in water. Giant oak trees may soar high above a forest floor where, long ago, green algae floated on the sunny surface of a pond. Now a squirrel scampers about the forest, hunting for acorns. But on that same spot, long long ago, a lazy frog once sat upon a lily pad, snapping up mosquitoes and soaking up the summer sun.

Index